God bless you.
Genesis 1:27
Joyce Wood

This Book Bee-longs To:

_____

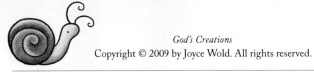

God's Creations
Copyright © 2009 by Joyce Wold. All rights reserved.

Published by Tate Publishing & Enterprises, LLC
127 E. Trade Center Terrace | Mustang, Oklahoma 73064 USA
1.888.361.9473 | www.tatepublishing.com

Tate Publishing is committed to excellence in the publishing industry. The company reflects the philosophy established by the founders, based on Psalm 68:11,
"The Lord gave the word and great was the company of those who published it."

Book design copyright © 2009 by Tate Publishing, LLC. All rights reserved.
Cover and Interior design by Ryan Palmer
Illustration by Kathy Hoyt

Published in the United States of America
ISBN: 978-1-61566-636-2
Juvenile Nonfiction: Religious: Christian: Learning Concepts
09.11.16

God's Creations

Written By Joyce Wold

TATE PUBLISHING & Enterprises

DEDICATION

To my precious grandchildren:
Naomi, Tyler, Annika, Audrey, and Kathryn

ACKNOWLEDGEMENT

Thank you
Bob for your encouragement,
Valerie and Steve, Natalie and Dan for your support.

God created a slow, slimy snail
And a wonderful, water-spouting
whale.

A wiggly, wobbly worm
And a smooth-soaring tern.

God created a busy, buzzing bee
And a tall, towering tree.

A slithery, scaly snake

And a rocking, rippling lake.

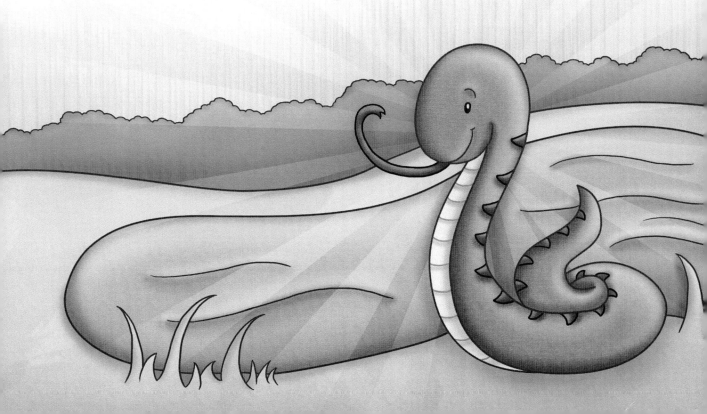

God created a floaty, floppy frog
And a darling, dapper dog.

A splishy, splashy shower
And a fragrant, frilly flower.

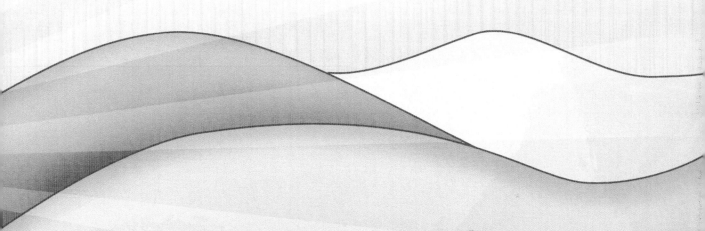

God created a super, sunny sky
And a fuzzy, frolicking fly.

Smooth, sinking sand
And lots and lots of land.

God created a big, brawny bear
And a happy, hoppity hare.

A honking, hollering goose
And a mighty, massive moose.

God created a mysterious, man-faced moon

And a brown, bushy baboon.

A mighty, majestic mountain
And a fabulous, frothy fountain.

God created a brilliant, bouncing boy
Jesting, jumping, and full of joy.

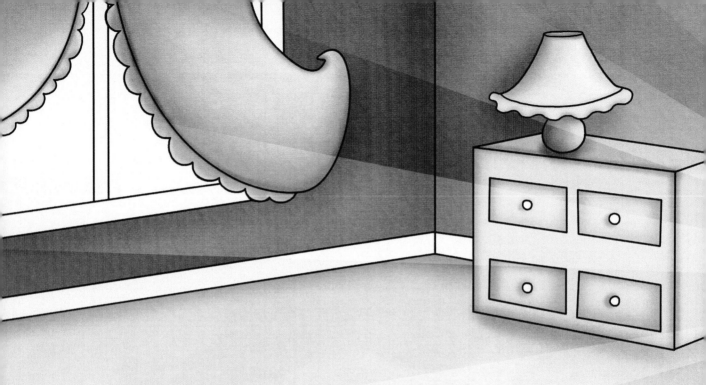

A great, glamorous girl
Like a precious, priceless pearl.

And best of all, God created you—

Clever, comical, and cuddly **you!**

Place your photo here

e|LIVE

listen|imagine|view|experience

AUDIO BOOK DOWNLOAD INCLUDED WITH THIS BOOK!

In your hands you hold a complete digital entertainment package. In addition to the paper version, you receive a free download of the audio version of this book. Simply use the code listed below when visiting our website. Once downloaded to your computer, you can listen to the book through your computer's speakers, burn it to an audio CD or save the file to your portable music device (such as Apple's popular iPod) and listen on the go!

How to get your free audio book digital download:

1. Visit www.tatepublishing.com and click on the e|LIVE logo on the home page.
2. Enter the following coupon code:

   8aa3-ebc1-ae68-7ecf-bdd7-8c3b-3d44-3d12
3. Download the audio book from your e|LIVE digital locker and begin enjoying your new digital entertainment package today!